Published by
MAE Dixon, LLC 311
Autumn Lake Dr
McDonough, GA 30253
(850) 554-4663

Other publications at maedixon.com

Copyright © 2022 Mae Dixon All rights reserved

This book or any portion thereof may not be reproduced or used in any manner whatsoever without the express permission of the publisher except in the use of brief quotations in a book review.

Requested permission must be in writing to
maedixon62@gmail.com

All Scripture taken from The Message (MSG); The NIV Bible; The KJV Bible/… Used by permission of NavPress Publishing Group

Published by MAE Dixon, ISBN - 978-1-7353725-6-3 ISBN – 978-17353725-7-0

I Lead With Authority Because I Can My Journal

It's a blueprint to help young men prepare for adulthood while experiencing their time as adolescents and into their teen years.

This journal offers real life and real time instruction in a language that boys can understand and apply to daily life.

This journal is one of the many tools used by the author as part of the Youth Leadership Development Program offered by A Will & Way, Inc.

Use each page to record your thoughts, the title is merely a thought to get you started, feel free to use your own. If you need more space add a sheet of paper. If you'd prefer to draw instead of writing do it. For more information about her other resources visit www.maedixon.com

This is His-Story
A Letter of Love

Greetings,

What is that you fancy most in this life? Is it your good looks, your swagger, toned body" Or is it the fact that underneath all of that there's a heart that ache for others more than oneself; a mind that is focused on making a difference in the world by stocking up on wisdom and knowledge.

Life can be a double -edged sword. On the one side everything is smooth and easy, there's not a care in the world. While, on the other hand there's much work and sacrifice to be had for the most basic accomplishments. When one has a full view of what's behind them, the present and what's happening now there is no need to apply oneself; no fret, no care, no effort... However, since we don't know what's before us and can only guess at the present at times; we should be diligent in preparing ourselves. Everything comes with a price.

Your birth cost someone something, if nothing more than the pain endured by your mother to get you here. For every decision you make, no matter your age, you must stop to consider the cost of that decision; at that moment and into the future. "If I do *this* (act) what will the consequences be?"

Right now a "moment" seems like a long time but I promise you, the time will be far greater and the consequences more costly if you fail to use it wisely.

I call you my brother because you are my brother (in love), and because I love you. I want you to live a long, happy and prosperous life. Trouble will come but because you will have attained (Godly) wisdom and knowledge it won't overwhelm you.

TABLE OF CONTENTS

Affirmations
Meditation
GIFT
8 Keys of Excellence
Integrity
Failure
Success
Purpose
Commitment
Ownership
Flexibility
Balance

AFFIRMATIONS

I am the head and not the tail

I was bought with a price (by God)

I will honor my mother, father and elders so that I may enjoy a long life

I am a leader not a follower

I am a child of the king.

I can do all things through Christ who gives me strength.

I am more than a conqueror.

To love myself is the greatest gift to the world.

I surround myself with people who affirm me.

My circle consist of those who lift me up.

I give more than I take.

The simplest prayer is, "Lord, help me."

We all must believe in something, let it be in a living God who protects and provide for our daily needs.

*All scriptural quotes taken from The Message (MSG); The NIV Bible; The KJV Bible

MEDITATION

When all else fails, seek peace within, doing so will give You clarity and a calm that surpasses all understanding.

"**Meditation** is a technique such as mindfulness, the focusing on a particular object, thought, activity to train attention and awareness, to achieve a mentally clear and emotionally calm and stable state." (Wikipedia)

Centering Prayer is a surrendering method of meditation, that reaches back to the early days of Christianity. To do this form of meditation:
- Find a quiet space where you are unlikely to be disturbed.
- Sit in a way that allows you to be relaxed in body and alert in mind. Use a chair, meditation cushion or prayer rug, according to your own physical needs and preferences.
- Gently close your eyes.• "Allow your heart to open toward that invisible but always present Origin (God)of all that exists " Whenever you become aware of a thought, no matter what its nature, let it go.

- Use a "sacred word". This is a word or short phrase that helps you to let go of thoughts. It is a reminder of your intention to remain open to the silence. Generally sacred words fall into one of 2 categories: "God" words/phrases such as "Abba", "Jesus, "Mary", "Reality", "Come Lord" or "state" words/phrases such as "love", "peace", "be still".
- Sacred words are not used as mantras, as in constantly repeating them, but as a reminder of your intention to remain open.

Continue this practice for 20 minutes. At the end of the time get up and go about your business, leaving the practice behind, in the same way you let go of your thoughts.

People who are just beginning, and are particularly restless in mind and body, may find it easier to start off with shorter prayer periods, perhaps only 5 minutes per sit to start. Then after a few days extend the time to 10 minutes and so on until you are able to sit for 20 minutes. Give the practice at least 2 weeks before you decide if it is right for you.• Two 20-30 minute sits per day are considered ideal. It is

strongly recommended that no one meditates for more the 60 minutes a day unless you are attending a structured retreat with expert. -Source:
<u>CONTEMPLATIVE.ORG</u>

GIFT

You have a gift called "Youth" right now. Use it wisely, be smart, be generous with your love to your fellow man but, love and respect yourself *first* .

Spend wisely. Let your adornment be a healthy body and the beauty will shine through. Things do not bring happiness, peace nor joy, nor does it make the person, but people who love you do. Achieve great things, you were born for a purpose, you have a gift(s) that is unique to you. Find out what it is and use it/them to the fullest potential.

Don't allow others to bring you down to their level. If they're not willing to step up then leave them where they are. You are destined for greatness and don't allow anyone to distract you. Don't confuse greatness with money or fame, greatness comes from within and is everlasting. Money comes from the world and is most often temporal. There's many a bum who is filled with greatness but lost their way because they allowed money and fame to define and corrupt them.

Wait for love - don't be in a hurry to find a girlfriend, Take the time to know who you are and then to know who she is. The girlfriend/mate for you has already been determined, there is no need to experiment with every girl that makes herself available. You will find her and she will bring with her the ingredients for a real love relationship. The acceptance of anything less is a prescription for disaster.

Ms Mae

MY JOURNAL

I'm writing my own story. The rest of this Journal is designed to encourage, inspire and motivate me to document my personal journey as I navigate this thing called life each day. In doing so I will find that life is less stressful when I take the time to write down my thoughts.

Sometimes I may find it helpful to just write mindlessly, walk away and then return later to see what was written and determine if I still feel that way. My journal is a judgement - free zone. If I feel troubled by some of the things I think or write I won't be afraid to talk about it with someone I trust such as a parent, aunt, mentor, best friend or doctor.

Life is not about regrets, but preparations.

A Life well lived is GOLDEN.

_____
_____
___ _____
_____
_____
___ ___ _____
_____
_____
___ _____ _____
_____
_____
_____
_____
___ _____
_____
___ _____
_____
_____
_____
_____
_____
_____
__ _____

Strangers stab you in the back, girlfriends stab you in the heart, but true friends poke each other with straws.

We are born into this world not to be perfect, but to be ourselves.

I'm handsome. I'm strong. I'm unique. I won't let anyone tell me otherwise.

_____
_____
_____
_____
_____
_____
_____
_____
_____
_____
_____
_____
_____
_____
_____
_____
_____
_____
_____

Everyone is born with the same amount of potential, it's up to you to decide what to do with it.

Maybe you have to let go of who you were to become who you are meant to be!

_____

_____

_____

_____

_____

_____

_____

_____

_____

_____

_____

_____

_____

_____

_____

_____

_____

_____

_____

It hurts when your friend gets a girlfriend and then they slowly forget about everyone else.

_____
_____
_____
_____
_____
_____
_____
_____
_____
_____
_____
_____
_____
_____
_____

A girls' laugh is much more cheerful than a boy's. But a boys' tears are much more meaningful than a girl's.

If people are trying to bring you down, it means you're above THEM.

Sometimes I just want to be alone, but people start talking to me.

— — — — — — — — — — — —
— — — — — — — — — — — —
— — — — — — — — — — — —
— — — — — — — — — — — —
— — — — — — — — — — — —
— — — — — — — — — — — —
— — — — — — — — — — — —
— — — — — — — — — — — —
— — — — — — — — — — — —
— — — — — — — — — — — —
— — — — — — — — — — — —
— — — — — — — — — — — —
— — — — — — — — — — — —
— — — — — — — — — — — —
— — — — — — — — — — — —
— — — — — — — — — — — —

I'm single not because I don't pray for love. I'm single because I don't play with love.

_ _ _ _ _ _ _ _ _ _ _
_ _ _ _ _ _ _ _ _ _ _
_ _ _ _ _ _ _ _ _ _ _
_ _ _ _ _ _ _ _ _ _ _
_ _ _ _ _ _ _ _ _ _ _
_ _ _ _ _ _ _ _ _ _ _
_ _ _ _ _ _ _ _ _ _ _
_ _ _ _ _ _ _ _ _ _ _
_ _ _ _ _ _ _ _ _ _ _
_ _ _ _ _ _ _ _ _ _ _
_ _ _ _ _ _ _ _ _ _ _
_ _ _ _ _ _ _ _ _ _ _
_ _ _ _ _ _ _ _ _ _ _
_ _ _ _ _ _ _ _ _ _ _
_ _ _ _ _ _ _ _ _ _ _
_ _ _ _ _ _ _ _ _ _ _
_ _ _ _ _ _ _ _ _ _ _

Be careful of who you trust, the devil was once an angel.

Deep down we all need that one person. No matter how much we deny it. It's a fact that remains.

There are no hopeless situations.
Only people who think
hopelessly.

― ― ― ― ― ― ― ― ― ― ― ― ―
― ― ― ― ― ― ― ― ― ― ― ― ―
― ― ― ― ― ― ― ― ― ― ― ― ―
― ― ― ― ― ― ― ― ― ― ― ― ―
― ― ― ― ― ― ― ― ― ― ― ― ―
― ― ― ― ― ― ― ― ― ― ― ― ―
― ― ― ― ― ― ― ― ― ― ― ― ―
― ― ― ― ― ― ― ― ― ― ― ― ―
― ― ― ― ― ― ― ― ― ― ― ― ―
― ― ― ― ― ― ― ― ― ― ― ― ―
― ― ― ― ― ― ― ― ― ― ― ― ―
― ― ― ― ― ― ― ― ― ― ― ― ―
― ― ― ― ― ― ― ― ― ― ― ― ―
― ― ― ― ― ― ― ― ― ― ― ― ―
― ― ― ― ― ― ― ― ― ― ― ― ―
― ― ― ― ― ― ― ― ― ― ― ― ―
― ― ― ― ― ― ― ― ― ― ― ― ―

I hate it when I'm bored and there isn't anything on TV, but when I'm busy, everything comes on.

You hurt me... so why do I still love you?

_____
_____
_____
_____
_____
_____
_____
_____
_____
_____
_____
_____
_____
_____
_____
_____
_____
_____

Not wanting to talk to anyone, but at the same time not wanting to be alone....

Give thanks for what you are now, and keep fighting for what you want to be tomorrow.

Things will happen in your life that you can't stop. There's a purpose for the good and for the bad.

Don't judge me for who my friends are, we are different people.

Goodbyes make you think. They make you realize what you've lost, what you have and what you took for granted.

If a boy and girl are talking, smiling and laughing together, doesn't mean they are together! They can be just good friends.

A best friend is someone you grow up with.... A true friend is someone who helps you grow up.

Sorry, my room is a mess

I miss school during the summer, and I miss summer during school.

My best friend and I can speak to each other through facial expressions.

Life is nothing but challenges; the more you undergo, the more you learn.

There's only one panacea for
ALL our worries.... GOD.

I had a crush on a girl, and she was already taken. I guess it was never meant to be.

Life throws sticks and stones at you, but they help you become who you are today.

A good life should always be made, not to be waited for.

Who am I?

— — — — — — — — —
— — — — — — — — —
— — — — — — — — —
— — — — — — — — —
— — — — — — — — —
— — — — — — — — —
— — — — — — — — —
— — — — — — — — —
— — — — — — — — —
— — — — — — — — —
— — — — — — — — —
— — — — — — — — —
— — — — — — — — —
— — — — — — — — —

My Aspirations Are.

Things I need to do to achieve my Aspirations are

_____

In life being fair or unfair depends on how we think, we are equally the same, we breathe in the same air, we look upon the same sky and we stand on the same ground. What makes us different is our perception in life. How we're going to cope with the difficulties of life.

The thing you think isn't working for you is all part of everything working for you.
Abraham Hicks

Don't make yourself small for anyone. Be the awkward, funny, intelligent, beautiful little weirdo that you are.

Be the best you you can be.

NOTES

NOTES

A drawing of my most prized possession:

Author Bio

Mae Dixon is the Amazon best-selling author of "The Secret Code of Girls – The Ins & Outs of Being a Female," " The Secret Code of Girls - Empowering Girls to Become Confident Women and "Restored by Grace - A Journey Like No Other". Dixon has also authored teen journals, poems, blogs and newsletters.

Dixon has experienced a rewarding real estate career for over 40 years where she received numerous awards, public exposure (newspaper, magazines, podcasts & tv) for her expertise and peer leadership including Realtor of the Year and Top Gun in Real Estate. She is a certified spiritual healing coach and has written and facilitated numerous empowerment programs for women and youth.

Dixon is a community advocate for survivors of domestic violence and social justice. She has founded and served on numerous boards and committees and received awards and recognition for her leadership. Dixon is the proud mother of two sons who blessed her with many grand and great-grandchildren.

Prior Work Dixon has presided over and served on the Pensacola and Florida Real Estate Association Boards, The Community

Drug and Alcohol Commission, Pensacola-Escambia Citizens Law Enforcement Liaison Group, City of Clearwater Citizen's Academy, Pensacola Police Academy, Escambia County Sheriff's Academy, The Pensacola-Escambia Human Relations Commission, Escambia Board of Adjustments, Florida Supreme Court County Mediator,

Affiliations National Assn of Female Executives, National Assn of Women Council of Realtors, Recipient of Congressional Award and Points of Light Award

Opportunities are available to teach leadership development based upon this journal. For training or speaking engagements email maedixon62@gmail.com
or maedixon.com

OOPS!

Did you run out? No worries, order additional Journals for yourself, your family and friends At:maedixon62@gmail.com include the following information: Name, phone #, title of book/journal and quantity desired.

www.ingramcontent.com/pod-product-compliance
Lightning Source LLC
Chambersburg PA
CBHW071254070526
44583CB00017B/2466